DK READERS

LEARNING
TO READ
pre-level 1

Colourful Days

A Dorling Kindersley Book

blue

How many colours

A Note to Parents and Teachers

DK READERS is a compelling reading programme for children, designed in conjunction with leading literacy experts, including Cliff Moon M.Ed., Honorary Fellow of the University of Reading. Cliff Moon has spent many years as a teacher and teacher educator specializing in reading and has written more than 140 books for children and teachers. He reviews regularly for teachers' journals.

Beautiful illustrations and superb full-colour photographs combine with engaging, easy-to-read stories to offer a fresh approach to each subject in the series. Each DK READER is guaranteed to capture a child's interest while developing his or her reading skills, general knowledge, and love of reading.

The five levels of DK READERS are aimed at different reading abilities, enabling you to choose the books that are exactly right for your child:

Pre-level 1 – Learning to read
Level 1 – Beginning to read
Level 2 – Beginning to read alone
Level 3 – Reading alone
Level 4 – Proficient readers

The "normal" age at which a child begins to read can be anywhere from three to eight years old, so these levels are only a general guideline.

No matter which level you select, you can be sure that you are helping your child learn to read, then read to learn!

LONDON, NEW YORK, DELHI,
MUNICH AND MELBOURNE

Series Editor Deborah Lock
Senior Art Editor Tory Gordon-Harris
Design Assistant Sadie Thomas
Production Claire Pearson
DTP Designer Almudena Díaz

Reading Consultant
Cliff Moon, M.Ed.

Published in Great Britian by
Dorling Kindersley Limited
80, The Strand, London WC2R ORL
6 8 10 9 7 5

A Penguin Company

A CIP record for this book is available
from the British Library

ISBN 978-0-7513-4397-7

Colour reproduction by Colourscan, Singapore
Printed and bound in China by L Rex Printing Co., Ltd.

The publisher would like to thank the following for their kind permission
to reproduce their photographs:
a=above; c=centre; b=below; l=left; r=right t=top;

British Museum: 28br, 32br; **Corbis:** Bill Ross 8cl; Craig Tuttle 21br;
Jeremy Horner 4c; **Gables Travels:** 16-17; **Getty Images:** Jerry Driendl 10-
11; Darrell Gulin 8-9; Terry Husebye 26-27; Tom King 15tr; Mike Timo 6-
7; **Paul Goff:** 27bl; **Judith Miller & Dorling Kindersley & Bonhams,
Edinburgh:** 13bl; **Tracy Morgan:** 2crb, 8bl; **Natural History Museum:**
9bcr, 19bcl, 19bcl, 25br; **Stephen Oliver:** 2tr, 11bc, 12bc, 12br, 15bc, 18-
19, 19br, 26bl, 32c; **Guy Ryecart:** 17bc; Ross Simms and the Winchcombe
Folk & Police Museum: 2cra, 22bl; **Barrie Watts:** 2br, 7br; **Jerry Young:**
22-23, 24-25, 25c, 32bl

All other images © Dorling Kindersley.
For further imformation see: www.dkimages.com

see our complete catalogue at
www.dk.com

green

yellow

pink

red

Come and
play with me.

can you see?

5

nose

snow

white

6

~eye

We can play
in the cold,
white snow.

We can look at
the purple flowers.

leaf

purple

flower

9

blossom

We can run round the trees with the pink blossoms.

pink

petal

rabbit

grey

12

ear

fur

We can play
with the small,
grey rabbits.

We can look at
the boats on the
blue sea.

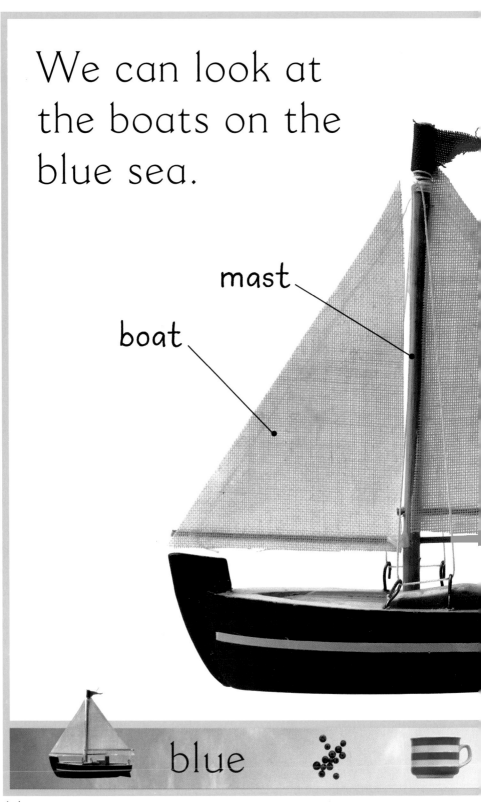

mast

boat

blue

14

sea

We can run round the tall, yellow sunflowers.

yellow

sunflower

petal

orange

We can
eat a cold,
orange lolly.

lolly

stick

leaf

red

We can kick the red leaves and pick the red apples.

apple

jaw

beetle

black

22

ant

We can look
at the ants and
the black beetle.

frog

feet

brown

We can croak
like the small,
brown frogs.

tree

needles

 green

We can run round
the tall, green trees.

We can hang up
silver balls and
put on gold crowns.

silver

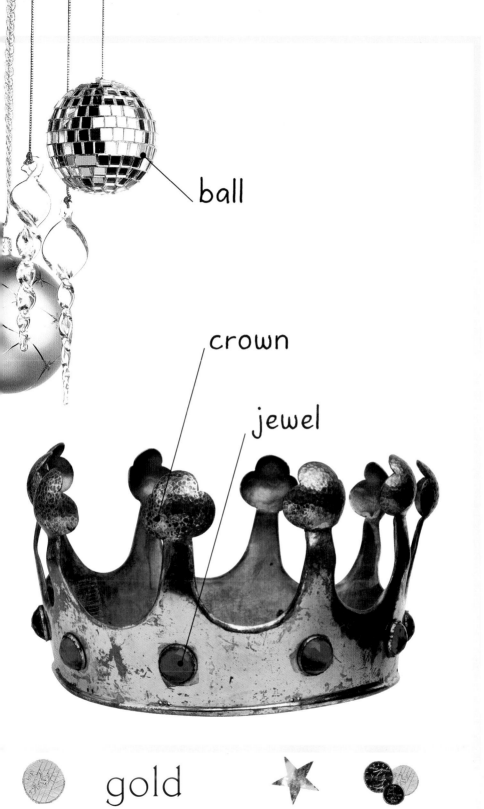

ball

crown

jewel

 gold

How many colours

can you see?

Picture word list

white
page 6

purple
page 8

pink
page 10

grey
page 12

blue
page 14

yellow
page 16

orange
page 18

red
page 20

black
page 22

brown
page 24

green
page 26

silver and gold
page 28